Spanish Short Stories for Beginners
Book 5

Over 100 Dialogues and Daily Used Phrases to Learn Spanish in Your Car. Have Fun & Grow Your Vocabulary, with Crazy Effective Language Learning Lessons

www.LearnLikeNatives.com

www.LearnLikeNatives.com

© Copyright 2020

By Learn Like A Native

ALL RIGHTS RESERVED

No part of this book may be reproduced, stored in a retrieval system, or transmitted in any form or by any means, without the prior written permission of the publisher.

www.LearnLikeNatives.com

TABLE OF CONTENT

INTRODUCTION	5
CHAPTER 1 New Roommates	
/ Common everyday objects + possession	17
Translation of the Story	34
New Roommates	34
CHAPTER 2 A Day in the Life	
/ transition words	45
Translation of the Story	60
A Day in the Life	60
CHAPTER 3 The Camino Inspiration	
/ Numbers + Family	71
Translation of the Story	86
The Camino Inspiration	86
CONCLUSION	95
About the Author	101

www.LearnLikeNatives.com

www.LearnLikeNatives.com

INTRODUCTION

Before we dive into some Spanish, I want to congratulate you, whether you're just beginning, continuing, or resuming your language learning journey. Here at Learn Like a Native, we understand the determination it takes to pick up a new language and after reading this book, you'll be another step closer to achieving your language goals.

As a thank you for learning with us, we are giving you free access to our 'Speak Like a Native' eBook. It's packed full of practical advice and insider tips on how to make language learning quick, easy, and most importantly, enjoyable. Head over to LearnLikeNatives.com to access your free guide and peruse our huge selection of language learning resources.

Learning a new language is a bit like cooking—you need several different ingredients and the right technique, but the end result is sure to be delicious. We created this book of short stories for learning Spanish because language is alive. Language is about the senses—hearing, tasting the words on your tongue, and touching another culture up close. Learning a language in a classroom is a fine place to start, but it's not a complete introduction to a language.

In this book, you'll find a language come to life. These short stories are miniature immersions into the Spanish language, at a level that is perfect for beginners. This book is not a lecture on grammar. It's not an endless vocabulary list. This book is the closest you can come to a language immersion without leaving the country. In the stories within, you will see people speaking to each other, going through daily life situations, and using the most common, helpful words and phrases in language.

You are holding the key to bringing your Spanish studies to life.

Made for Beginners

We made this book with beginners in mind. You'll find that the language is simple, but not boring. Most of the book is in the present tense, so you will be able to focus on dialogues, root verbs, and understand and find patterns in subject-verb agreement.

This is not "just" a translated book. While reading novels and short stories translated into Spanish is a wonderful thing, beginners (and even novices) often run into difficulty. Literary licenses and complex sentence structure can make reading in your second language truly difficult—not to mention BORING. That's why Spanish Short

Stories for Beginners is the perfect book to pick up. The stories are simple, but not infantile. They were not written for children, but the language is simple so that beginners can pick it up.

The Benefits of Learning a Second Language

If you have picked up this book, it's likely that you are already aware of the many benefits of learning a second language. Besides just being fun, knowing more than one language opens up a whole new world to you. You will be able to communicate with a much larger chunk of the world. Opportunities in the workforce will open up, and maybe even your day-to-day work will be improved. Improved communication can also help you expand your business. And from a neurological perspective, learning a second language is like taking your daily vitamins and eating well, for your brain!

How To Use The Book

The chapters of this book all follow the same structure:

- A short story with several dialogs
- A summary in Spanish
- A list of important words and phrases and their English translation
- Questions to test your understanding
- Answers to check if you were right
- The English translation of the story to clear every doubt

www.LearnLikeNatives.com

You may use this book however is comfortable for you, but we have a few recommendations for getting the most out of the experience. Try these tips and if they work for you, you can use them on every chapter throughout the book.

1) Start by reading the story all the way through. Don't stop or get hung up on any particular words or phrases. See how much of the plot you can understand in this way. We think you'll get a lot more of it than you may expect, but it is completely normal not to understand everything in the story. You are learning a new language, and that takes time.

2) Read the summary in Spanish. See if it matches what you have understood of the plot.

3) Read the story through again, slower this time. See if you can pick up the meaning of any words or phrases you don't understand by using context clues and the information from the summary.

4) Test yourself! Try to answer the five comprehension questions that come at the end of each story. Write your answers down, and then check them against the answer key. How did you do? If you didn't get them all, no worries!

5) Look over the vocabulary list that accompanies the chapter. Are any of these the words you did not understand? Did you already know the meaning of some of them from your reading?

6) Now go through the story once more. Pay attention this time to the words and phrases you haven't understand. If you'd like, take the time to look them up to

expand your meaning of the story. Every time you read over the story, you'll understand more and more.

7) Move on to the next chapter when you are ready.

Read and Listen

The audio version is the best way to experience this book, as you will hear a native Spanish speaker tell you each story. You will become accustomed to their accent as you listen along, a huge plus for when you want to apply your new language skills in the real world.

If this has ignited your language learning passion and you are keen to find out what other resources are available, go to LearnLikeNatives.com,

www.LearnLikeNatives.com

where you can access our vast range of free learning materials. Don't know where to begin? An excellent place to start is our 'Speak Like a Native' free eBook, full of practical advice and insider tips on how to make language learning quick, easy, and most importantly, enjoyable.

And remember, small steps add up to great advancements! No moment is better to begin learning than the present.

www.LearnLikeNatives.com

FREE BOOK!

Get the *FREE BOOK* that reveals the secrets path to learn any language fast, and without leaving your country.

Discover:

- The **language 5 golden rules** to master languages at will

- Proven **mind training techniques** to revolutionize your learning

- A complete step-by-step guide to **conquering any language**

www.LearnLikeNatives.com

www.LearnLikeNatives.com

www.LearnLikeNatives.com

CHAPTER 1
New Roommates / Common everyday objects + possession

HISTORIA

Hoy es día de mudanza en la universidad. Los estudiantes de primer año trasladan **sus** cosas al dormitorio.

Anna llega a la universidad con sus padres. **Su** coche está cargado de **cajas**. Anna trae todo lo que necesita para un año de escuela con ella. Aparcan fuera del dormitorio de Anna. El edificio es un gran edificio de ladrillo. Se ve aburrido. Anna trata de pensar positivo. Este año será genial, se dice a sí misma.

Su familia comienza a descargar el coche. Anna está muy preparada. Sacan cajas llenas de sus cosas. Su hermano la ayuda a llevar las cajas a la habitación. La habitación es pequeña. Hay dos camas. Anna tendrá un compañero de cuarto.

La primera caja que Anna abre tiene material escolar. Ella pone sus **blocs de notas**, **lápices** y **bolígrafos** en su escritorio. La habitación no tiene decoración, a excepción de un **televisor** en la pared. Anna organiza sus cosas en la habitación. Ella saca su **calendario** para ponerlo en la pared.

"¡Esto no es **mío**!", dice. Es un calendario de mujeres guapas.

"Esto es **tuyo**", dice Anna, señalando a su hermano.

"Oh, lo siento", dice su hermano. Anna lo tira a la **basura**. La familia se ríe.

Llaman a la puerta. Abren la puerta. Una chica rubia está afuera. Está con una mujer mayor, su madre.

"Hola, soy Beatriz", dice la chica.

"Soy Anna", dice Anna. "¡Supongo que somos compañeras de cuarto!"

"¿De dónde eres?", pregunta Beatriz.

"Cerca, a sólo una hora al norte", dice Anna.

"¡Yo también!", dice Beatriz.

Las chicas se dan la mano y sonríen. Beatriz trae sus propias cajas. Las familias ayudan a sus hijas a desempacar.

Los primeros días de escuela son agradables. Anna hace nuevos amigos. Ella y Beatriz se llevan muy bien. Anna va a sus nuevas clases. Todo es perfecto. Sin embargo, una cosa está mal. Algunas de las pertenencias de Anna comienzan a desaparecer. Primero, ella no puede encontrar su **cepillo**. Luego, al día siguiente, se mira en el **espejo**. Ve su **loción**, pero su **perfume** ha desaparecido. Cuando ella llega de clase esa noche, pone algo de música. No hay sonido. ¡Su **altavoz** no está!

Le pregunta a Beatriz. "Beatriz", dice. "¿Tú has perdido algo?"

"¡Sí!" dice Beatriz. "Mi **computadora portátil**. Me estoy volviendo loca."

"¡Oh no!", dice Anna. "También me faltan algunas cosas."

A Anna le faltan tres cosas ahora. Ella llama a su madre por su **celular**.

"Hola, mamá", dice Anna.

"Hola, cariño", dice su madre. "¿Cómo va la escuela?"

"Bien", dice Anna. "Pero mis pertenencias siguen desapareciendo."

"¿Qué quieres decir?" pregunta su madre. Anna le dice a su madre sobre el perfume, el altavoz, y el cepillo perdido.

"Eso es tan extraño", dice su madre. "¿Los llevaste a algún lado?"

"No, mamá", dice Anna. "Nunca salí de la habitación. El resto del **equipo de música** está aquí. Mi **reproductor de mp3**, también."

"¿Cierras la puerta?" le pregunta su madre.

"¡Sí, mamá!" dice Anna. "Y es sólo el perfume que no está. ¡Todavía tengo todo el **maquillaje**, **lápiz labial**, todo!"

"¿Crees que podría ser Beatriz?", le pregunta su madre.

"De ninguna manera, ella también está perdiendo cosas", dice Anna.

"Vale, ve a ver a los objetos perdidos", dice la madre de Anna.

"¡Bien! Tengo que irme", dice Anna.

Anna cuelga el teléfono. La idea de su madre es buena. Baja las escaleras a la oficina del dormitorio. Pide ver la caja de objetos perdidos. La caja está llena. Mira dentro de ella. Encuentra **cuadernos**, una **cámara de vídeo** e incluso un **peine**. Pero no ve sus cosas. Se ve más. Ve una **computadora portátil**.

"¿Es **tuyo**?", pregunta pensando en Beatriz. Lo saca. Lo es. Toma el ordenador para dárselo a Beatriz. Al menos encuentra algo.

Sube las escaleras. Le da la computadora a Beatriz.

"¡Wow, Anna, es **mi** computadora!" dice Beatriz. "Muchas gracias."

"De nada", dice Anna. "Me alegra haber encontrado **tu** computadora."

"Yo también", dice Beatriz. "¿Encontraste alguna de tus cosas?"

"No", dice Anna.

"Triste", dice Beatriz. Las chicas se van a dormir.

Al día siguiente, Beatriz tiene clase. Anna se queda en el dormitorio. Trabaja en un proyecto, usando

tijeras para cortar cuadros para pegar en una **carpeta**. Piensa en sus objetos perdidos. Quizás debería mirar en el dormitorio. Mira por todas partes. Luego se vuelve hacia el armario de Beatriz. Lo abre. Mira dentro de él.

"¡Esto es mío!", dice Anna. Saca su cepillo. Está sorprendida. ¿Por qué está su cepillo en el armario de Beatriz? Mira más de cerca. Debajo de una pila de **ropa**, siente algo duro. Lo saca. ¡Es su botella de perfume! Cuando mira más de cerca, también encuentra su altavoz.

"Era Beatriz todo el tiempo", dice Anna. Suena el **teléfono** de la habitación. Anna responde. Es la mamá de Beatriz.

"Hola, Anna", dice la mamá de Beatriz. "¿Cómo estás?"

"Bien", dice Anna. "Beatriz no está aquí."

"¿Puedes decirle que llamé?" le pregunta la madre de Beatriz.

"Sí, pero, ¿puedo hablarte de algo?" pregunta Anna.

"Claro", dice la mamá de Beatriz.

"Algunas de mis cosas han desaparecido", dice Anna. "Y acabo de encontrar muchas de ellas en el armario de **su** hija."

"Oh, no", dice la mamá de Beatriz. "Necesito decirte algo."

"¿Qué?", dice Anna.

"Beatriz es una cleptómana", dice su madre. "Toma cosas y luego las devuelve exactamente siete días después. Ella te devolverá esos objetos para mañana."

"¿Qué hago?", pregunta Anna.

"Espera a que ella los devuelva", dice su madre.

"Está bien", dice Anna.

"Gracias por entenderlo", dice la madre de Beatriz.

RESUMEN

Anna y Beatriz son compañeras de cuarto. Es su primer año en la universidad. Se encuentran en el día de la mudanza. Consiguen su dormitorio establecido. Sus padres ayudan. Se llevan bien. Durante la primera semana, muchas de las posesiones de Anna desaparecen. No las puede encontrar en ninguna parte. Beatriz también tiene algunos objetos que faltan. Anna busca por todas partes. Busca en los objetos perdidos, donde encuentra el ordenador de Beatriz desaparecido. Cuando Beatriz no está, Anna mira en su armario. Encuentra todos sus objetos. Llama la madre de Beatriz. Le dice a Anna que Beatriz es una cleptómana.

Lista de Vocabulario

their	su (3ra persona)
her	su (femenino)
boxes	cajas
mine	mío
notepads	blocs de notas
pencils	lápices
pens	bolígrafos
television	televisión

calendar	calendario
his	su (masculino)
trash can	bote de basura
brush	cepillo
mirror	espejo
lotion	loción
perfume	perfume
speaker	altavoz
computer	computadora
cell phone	teléfono celular
stereo system	sistema estéreo
makeup	maquillaje
lipstick	pintalabios
notebook	cuaderno
video camera	cámara de vídeo
comb	peine

my	mi
yours	tus / sus
your	tu / su
scissors	tijeras
clothes	ropa
telephone	telefono
your	tu / su

PREGUNTAS

1) ¿Cómo se conocen Beatriz y Anna?

    a) siempre han sido amigas

    b) se reúnen en clase

    c) son compañeras de cuarto

    d) van a la misma escuela

2) ¿Cuál de estos artículos no desapareció?

a) cepillo

b) perfume

c) altavoz

d) espejo

3) ¿Qué sugiere la madre de Anna?

    a) que Anna vuelva a casa

    b) que Anna se enfrente a Beatriz

    c) que Anna compre un nuevo cepillo

    d) que Anna busque en los objetos perdidos

4) ¿Qué encuentra Anna en los objetos perdidos?

    a) su cepillo

    b) la computadora de Beatriz

    c) una sudadera

    d) su perfume

5) ¿Qué pasó con las cosas de Anna?

    a) Beatriz las tomó y las puso en su armario

    b) Anna las perdió

    c) Anna las tiró

    d) nada

RESPUESTAS

1) ¿Cómo se conocen Beatriz y Anna?

    c) son compañeras de cuarto

2) ¿Cuál de estos artículos no desapareció?

    d) espejo

3) ¿Qué sugiere la madre de Anna?

    d) que Anna busque en los objetos perdidos

4) ¿Qué encuentra Anna en los objetos perdidos?

    b) la computadora de Beatriz

5) ¿Qué pasó con las cosas de Anna?

    a) Beatriz las tomó y las puso en su armario

Translation of the Story

New Roommates

STORY

Today is move-in day at the university. First year students move **their** things into the dormitory.

Anna arrives to the university with her parents. **Her** car is loaded with **boxes**. Anna brings everything she needs for a year of school with her. They park outside of Anna's dormitory. The building is a big, brick building. It looks boring. Anna tries to think positive. This year will be great, she tells herself.

Her family begins to unload the car. Anna is very prepared. They take out boxes full of her things. Her brother helps her take the boxes up to the room. The room is small. There are two beds. Anna will have a roommate.

The first box Anna opens has school supplies. She puts her **notepads**, **pencils** and **pens** on her desk. The room has no decoration, except for a **television** on the wall. Anna organizes her things in the room. She takes her **calendar** out to put on the wall.

"This isn't **mine**!" she says. It is a calendar of pretty women.

"This is **his**," Anna says, pointing at her brother.

"Oh, sorry," says her brother. Anna throws it in the **trash can**. The family laughs.

There is a knock on the door. They open the door. A blonde girl stands outside. She is with an older woman, her mother.

"Hello, I'm Beatriz," says the girl.

"I'm Anna," says Anna. "I guess we are roommates!"

"Where are you from?" asks Beatriz.

"Nearby, just an hour north," says Anna.

"Me too!" says Beatriz.

The girls shake hands and smile. Beatriz brings her own boxes. The families help their daughters unpack.

The first days of school are nice. Anna makes new friends. She and Beatriz get along great. Anna goes to her new classes. Everything is perfect. However, one thing is wrong. Some of Anna's belongings begin to disappear. First, she can't find her **brush**. Then, the next day, she looks in the **mirror**. She sees her **lotion** but her **perfume** is missing. When she arrives from class that evening, she puts on some music. There is no sound. Her **speaker** is gone!

She asks Beatriz. "Beatriz," she says. "Are you missing anything?"

"Yes!" says Beatriz. "My laptop **computer**. I am freaking out."

"Oh no!" says Anna. "I am missing a few things, too."

Anna is missing three things now. She calls her mother on her **cell phone**.

"Hi, mom," says Anna.

"Hi, honey," says her mom. "How is school?"

"Fine," says Anna. "But my belongings keep disappearing."

"What do you mean?" asks her mom. Anna tells her mom about the missing perfume, the missing speaker, and the missing brush.

"That is so strange," says her mom. "Did you take them somewhere?"

"No, mom," says Anna. "I never left the room. The rest of the **stereo system** is here. My **mp3 player,** too."

"Do you lock your door?" asks her mom.

"Yes, mom!" says Anna. "And it's just the perfume that is gone. I still have all the other **makeup**, **lipstick**, everything!"

"Do you think it could be Beatriz?" asks her mom.

"No way, she is missing stuff too," says Anna.

"Ok, go check the lost-and-found," says Anna's mom.

"Ok! Gotta go," says Anna.

Anna hangs up the phone. Her mom's idea is good. She goes downstairs to the dormitory office. She asks to see the lost-and-found box. The box is full. She looks through it. She finds **notebooks**, a **video camera**, and even a **comb**. But does not see her things. She looks more. She sees a laptop **computer**.

"Is that **yours**?" she asks, thinking of Beatriz. She pulls it out. It is. She takes the computer to give to Beatriz. At least she finds something.

She goes upstairs. She gives Beatriz the computer.

"Wow, Anna, it's **my** computer!" says Beatriz. "Thank you so much."

"You're welcome," says Anna. "So glad I found **your** computer."

"Me too," says Beatriz. "Did you find any of your things?"

"No," says Anna.

"Bummer," says Beatriz. The girls go to sleep.

The next day, Beatriz has class. Anna stays in the dorm room. She works on a project, using **scissors** to cut pictures to glue on a **folder**. She thinks about her missing items. Maybe she should look in the dorm room. She looks everywhere. Then she turns to Beatriz's closet. She opens it. She looks inside it.

"This is mine!" says Anna. She pulls out her brush. She is shocked. Why is her brush in Beatriz's closet? She looks closer. Under a stack of **clothes**, she feels something hard. She pulls it out. It is her bottle of perfume! When she looks closer, she finds her speaker, too.

"It was Beatriz the whole time," says Anna. The room **telephone** rings. Anna answers. It is Beatriz's mom.

"Hi, Anna," says Beatriz's mom. "How are you?"

"Fine," says Anna. "Beatriz isn't here."

"Can you tell her I called?" asks Beatriz's mom.

"Yes, but, can I talk to you about something?" asks Anna.

"Sure," says Beatriz's mom.

"Some of my things have gone missing," says Anna. "And I just found many of them in **your** daughter's closet."

"Oh, no," says Beatriz's mom. "I need to tell you something."

"What?" says Anna.

"Beatriz is a kleptomaniac," says her mom. "She takes things and then returns them exactly seven days later. She will return those items to you by tomorrow."

"What do I do?" asks Anna.

"Just wait for her to return them," says her mom.

"Okay," says Anna.

"Thank you for understanding," says Beatriz's mom.

CHAPTER 2
A Day in the Life / transition words

HISTORIA

Bey se despierta en una habitación de hotel. Está cansada. Su cuerpo está cansado, **pero** su mente está más cansada. Se siente sola. Sus amigos y familiares no entienden lo que es ser famoso. Ella se ríe. Quieren ser famosos. Quieren pasar un día en su vida. La gente piensa que las celebridades se divierten todo el día. Piensan que las celebridades consiguen lo que quieren. **Sin embargo**, Bey sabe que esto no es verdad.

¿Por qué la gente quiere ser famosa? Piensa Bey. Ella hace un café. Los medios de comunicación la muestran como éxito. La gente quiere éxito. Quieren una vida perfecta. **Como resultado**, intentan hacerse famosos. Ella sabe que la vida no es perfecta.

El reloj marca las siete en punto. Su día está ocupado. **Por lo tanto**, tiene que despertarse temprano. Algunas personas piensan que las celebridades duermen hasta tarde. Tiene mucho que hacer. No hay tiempo para dormir hasta tarde. Ella escucha el timbre.

"Hola", dice Bey.

"Hola, Bey", dicen las tres mujeres. Una mujer es su estilista. Otra mujer es su maquilladora. **Por último**, entra el peluquero. Ella abre la puerta. Van adentro. Empiezan a trabajar.

"¿Qué camisa?", dice el estilista.

"¿De qué color es el lápiz labial?" pregunta el maquillador.

"¿Por qué dormiste con el pelo así?", pregunta el peluquero.

El café de Bey se enfrió. Hace otro café. **Entonces**, ella responde a todas las preguntas. Le ayudan. **Finalmente**, está lista.

Sale del hotel a las 10 a.m. Hay mucha gente afuera. La esperan. Cuando sale, gritan. Toman fotos. Bey se mete en un coche. El coche tiene ventanas oscuras. Nadie puede ver dentro. **Por lo tanto**, ella puede hacer lo que quiera. Se relaja. Su teléfono suena.

"¿Hola?", dice ella.

"Bey, ¿dónde estás?" pregunta su representante.

"En el coche", dice.

"¡Llegas tarde!", dice el representante.

"Lo siento", dijo Bey. Tiene práctica de baile, clases de voz, y una sesión de fotos. Un día ocupado. Su representante mantiene su horario. Él le dice qué hacer y cuándo irse. Ella se siente atrapada. Debe trabajar para seguir siendo famosa. No puede tomarse unas vacaciones.

El coche se detiene. **Primero**, Bey tiene una sesión de fotos. Es para una revista. Una chica le pone maquillaje a Bey. Ella es un fan. Sonríe.

"¿Cómo estás?", pregunta ella.

"Está bien", dice Bey.

"Soy tu fan", dice.

"Gracias", dice Bey.

"Yo también canto", dice la chica. Empolva la cara de Bey.

"¿En serio?" pregunta Bey. Está aburrida.

"Sí. ¡Quiero ser famosa!", dice la chica.

"¡Ser famoso es mucho trabajo!", dice Bey.

"¡No me importa!" dice la chica.

"¿Qué vas a hacer esta noche?", pregunta Bey.

"Cena con mi novio, un paseo por el parque, tal vez visitar un museo", dice la chica.

"Tengo trabajo, un concierto", dice Bey. "**De hecho**, tengo uno cada noche. No puedo ir al parque **porque** la gente me reconoce. No me dejan en paz."

"Oh", dice la chica. Ella termina el maquillaje.

"**Por ejemplo**, no puedo recordar una visita a un museo", dice Bey. Está lista. Toma sus fotos. Su vestido es glamoroso. Se ve hermosa y feliz. Se despide y se sube al coche.

Segundo, Bey tiene práctica de danza. Practica en un estudio de danza. Su profesor es profesional. Practican para el concierto. El concierto de esta noche es en un estadio en la ciudad de Nueva York. Olvida el baile de su canción más famosa. Practica durante dos horas. **Sin duda**, ella sabe bailar.

Tercero, Bey tiene lecciones de voz. Cantantes famosos necesitan lecciones. Las lecciones de voz les ayudan a cantar fácilmente. Esto es importante. **Después de todo**, cantar un concierto cada noche es difícil.

Después de la voz, ella come el almuerzo. Su asistente se lo trae. Aunque es rápido, es saludable. Tiene un batido y una ensalada. Pronto debe prepararse para el concierto.

Ella revisa su teléfono. Bey tiene otro asistente. Este asistente usa redes sociales. Ella pone fotos en Instagram y Facebook. **En última instancia**, a Bey le gusta ver por sí misma. Su nueva película tiene 1.000.000 de likes. No está mal, piensa. También tiene muchos comentarios. Algunos son malos, así que Bey apaga su teléfono. Trata de ser positiva.

En el coche, Bey llama a sus amigos. Habla con su madre. Habla en el coche ya que no tiene mucho tiempo. Está cansada. Tiene dolor de cabeza. Quizás pueda dormir la siesta. Mira su teléfono. Es demasiado tarde para dormir la siesta.

Mientras Bey se prepara, los fans esperan. Hacen una fila afuera. Están emocionados. Pagaron mucho dinero por las entradas.

Ahora le duele la garganta. Bebe té caliente. Si no puede cantar, los fans estarán tristes. Mira su teléfono. Tiene una foto guardada para estos momentos. Es sólo una carta.

"Querida Bey", dice ahí.

"Eres mi cantante favorita. Creo que eres increíble. Quiero ser como tú cuando crezca. Amor, Susy." Es de un fan de 7 años. Bey la recuerda. Ella sonríe. Hay cientos de chicas como Susy en el concierto. **Por esta razón**, ella actúa.

Eventualmente, el concierto termina.

Más y más fans piden el autógrafo de Bey. Sonríen. Toman fotos en su teléfono. Ella se imagina sus vidas. Van a fiestas. Ven amigos. Van a restaurantes. De cualquier manera, tienen libertad. Ella está celosa. **A pesar** de no ser famosos, tienen una vida mejor.

Ella piensa en la chica de maquillaje de hoy. Se pregunta, ¿qué está haciendo ahora? Bey piensa que tal vez ya se fue.

De repente, su teléfono hace un sonido.

Es un recordatorio para ir a la cama. Mañana es otro día ocupado.

RESUMEN

Bey es una celebridad. Ella es una famosa cantante de pop. La gente está celosa de su vida. Sin embargo, no es fácil. Su día comienza temprano. Sus tres asistentes vienen al hotel. Ellos la preparan. Entonces, tiene un día ocupado. Ella va a una sesión de fotos. La chica de maquillaje quiere ser famosa. Bey dice que no es tan genial. Bey practica danza y canto. Luego se prepara para su concierto. Se siente enferma. Sin embargo, ella lo hace para sus muchos fans. Se toma fotos y firma autógrafos. Se siente celosa de la vida normal de sus fans.

Lista de Vocabulario

www.LearnLikeNatives.com

but	pero
however	sin embargo
as a result	como resultado
therefore	por lo tanto
lastly	por último
then	entonces
finally	finalmente
therefore	por lo tanto
first	primero
in fact	de hecho
because	porque
for example	por ejemplo
second	segundo
without a doubt	sin duda
after all	después de todo
even though	aunque

ultimately	en última instancia
so	así que
since	desde que
while	mientras
if	si
for this reason	por esta razón
eventually.	eventualmente.
either way	de cualquier manera
despite	a pesar de
all of a sudden	de repente

PREGUNTAS

1) ¿Qué persona no va al hotel de Bey?

    a) un artista de maquillaje

b) un estilista

c) un fan

d) un peluquero

2) ¿Por qué la llama el representante de Bey?

    a) preguntar dónde está

    b) para despedirla

    c) para felicitarla

    d) preguntar cómo está

3) ¿Cuál es el trabajo de Bey?

    a) bailarina

    b) estrella del pop

    c) presentadora de talk show

    d) fotógrafa

4) ¿Qué hace Bey para ayudarla a cantar?

    a) ella bebe té

    b) ella va a clases de voz

    c) ella reza

    d) cruza los dedos

5) ¿Qué significa el sonido del teléfono al final de la historia?

    a) alguien está llamando

    b) es hora de tomar medicamentos

    c) una notificación de Instagram

    d) es hora de ir a la cama

RESPUESTAS

1) ¿Qué persona no va al hotel de Bey?

    c) un fan

2) ¿Por qué la llama el representante de Bey?

    a) preguntar dónde está

3) ¿Cuál es el trabajo de Bey?

    b) estrella del pop

4) ¿Qué hace Bey para ayudarla a cantar?

    b) ella va a clases de voz

5) ¿Qué significa el sonido del teléfono al final de la historia?

    d) es hora de ir a la cama

Translation of the Story

A Day in the Life

STORY

Bey wakes up in a hotel room. She is tired. Her body is tired, **but** her mind is more tired. She feels alone. Her friends and family don't understand what it is like to be famous. She laughs. They want to be famous. They want to spend a day in her life. People think celebrities have fun all day. They think celebrities get anything they want. **However,** Bey knows this is not true.

Why do people want to be famous? Bey thinks. She makes a coffee. The media shows her as success. People want success. They want a perfect life. **As a result,** they try to become famous. She knows life is not perfect.

The clock says seven o'clock. Her day is busy. **Therefore**, she has to wake up early. Some people think celebrities sleep late. She has a lot to do. There is no time to sleep late. She hears the doorbell.

"Hello," says Bey.

"Hi, Bey," say the three women. One woman is her stylist. Another woman is her makeup artist. **Lastly**, the hairdresser enters. She opens the door. They go inside. They begin to work.

"Which shirt?" says the stylist.

"Which color of lipstick?" asks the makeup artist.

"Why did you sleep with your hair like that?" asks the hairdresser.

Bey's coffee is cold. She makes another coffee. **Then**, she answers all the questions. They help her. **Finally,** she is ready.

She leaves the hotel at 10 a.m. There are many people outside. They wait for her. When she goes out, they scream. They take pictures. Bey gets in a car. The car has dark windows. No one can see in. **Therefore,** she can do what she wants. She relaxes. Her phone rings.

"Hello?" she says.

"Bey, where are you?" asks her manager.

"In the car," she says.

"You're late!" says the manager.

"Sorry," said Bey. She has dance practice, voice lessons, and a photo shoot. A busy day. Her manager keeps her schedule. He tells her what to do. He tells her when to go. She feels stuck. She must work to stay famous. She can't take a vacation.

The car stops. **First**, Bey has a photo shoot. It is for a magazine. A girl puts makeup on Bey. She is a fan. She smiles.

"How are you?" she asks.

"Fine," says Bey.

"I am your fan," she says.

"Thank you," says Bey.

"I sing, too," the girl says. She powders Bey's face.

"Really?" asks Bey. She is bored.

"Yes. I want to be famous!" says the girl.

"Being famous is a lot of work!" says Bey.

"I don't care!" says the girl.

"What are you doing tonight?" asks Bey.

"Dinner with my boyfriend, a walk in the park, maybe visit a museum," says the girl.

"I have work, a concert," says Bey. "**In fact,** I have one every night. I can't go out to the park **because** people recognize me. They don't leave me alone."

"Oh," says the girl. She finishes the makeup.

"**For example**, I can't remember a visit to a museum," says Bey. She is finished. She takes her pictures. Her dress is glamorous. She looks beautiful and happy. She says goodbye and gets in the car.

Second, Bey has dance practice. She practices in a dance studio. Her teacher is professional. They practice for the concert. Tonight's concert is in a stadium in New York City. She forgets the dance for her most famous song. She practices for two hours. **Without a doubt**, she knows the dance.

Third, Bey has voice lessons. Famous singers need lessons. Voice lessons help them sing easily. This is important. **After all,** singing a concert every night is difficult.

After voice, she eats lunch. Her assistant brings it to her. Even though it is quick, it is healthy. She has a smoothie and a salad. Soon she must prepare for the concert.

She checks her phone. Bey has another assistant. This assistant does social media. She puts pictures on Instagram and Facebook. **Ultimately**, Bey likes to see for herself. Her new picture has 1,000,000 likes. Not bad, she thinks. It also has many comments. Some are mean, **so** Bey turns off her phone. She tries to be positive.

In the car, Bey calls her friends. She talks to her mother. She talks in the car **since** she doesn't have much time. She is tired. She has a headache. Maybe she can nap. She looks at her phone. It is too late to nap.

While Bey gets ready, fans wait. They make a line outside. They are excited. They paid a lot of money for the tickets.

Now her throat hurts. She drinks warm tea. **If** she can't sing, the fans will be sad. She looks at her phone. She has a picture saved for these moments. It is a letter.

"Dear Bey," it says.

"You are my favorite singer. I think you are amazing. I want to be just like you when I grow up. Love, Susy." It is from a 7-year-old fan. Bey remembers her. She smiles. There are hundreds of girls like Susy at the concert. **For this reason,** she performs.

Eventually, the concert ends.

More and more fans ask for Bey's autograph. They smile. They take pictures on their phone. She imagines their lives. They go to parties. They see friends. They go to restaurants. **Either way**, they have freedom. She is jealous. **Despite** not being famous, they have better lives.

She thinks of the makeup girl from today. She wonders, what is she doing now? Bey thinks maybe she will quit.

All of a sudden, her phone makes a sound.

It is a reminder to go to bed. Tomorrow is another busy day.

www.LearnLikeNatives.com

CHAPTER 3
The Camino Inspiration / Numbers + Family

A Molly le encantan las aventuras.

Ella es el miembro más valiente de su **familia**, incluso más valiente que sus **dos hermanos**. A menudo va de campamento con su familia en el bosque. Este fin de semana, van juntos a la montaña. La luna brilla, los pájaros y los animales están tranquilos. Molly se sienta con sus hermanos y su **hermana** junto al fuego, hablando y jugando. Ven un murciélago volar sobre sus cabezas.

"¡Ewww!" grita la hermana de Molly.

"¡Un murciélago!" grita **uno** de los hermanos de Molly.

Entonces, **tres** murciélagos más vuelan sobre sus cabezas.

"¡Ahhh! ¡Busquemos a **mamá** y **papá**!" grita el otro hermano, John.

"Es sólo un murciélago", dice Molly.

Llegan más murciélagos, hasta que hay **ocho** que vuelan por encima. La hermana y los hermanos de Molly desaparecen en sus tiendas, asustados. Molly no se mueve. ¡Ella mira mientras los murciélagos giraban, ahora **diecinueve**, no, **veinte**!

"Hola, Molly", dice su **madre**, caminando detrás de su **padre** a la fogata.

"Vaya, seguro que hay muchos murciélagos alrededor de este bosque", dice su padre. "¿No tienes miedo?"

Molly agitó la cabeza y vio a los murciélagos volar hacia el cielo estrellado.

"¡Vamos a cenar!" dijo ella. Sus hermanos y su hermana salen de sus tiendas de campaña. La familia come junto al fuego. Les encanta acampar juntos.

Molly tiene **22** años. Acaba de graduarse de la universidad, donde estudió ingeniería. No ha encontrado trabajo en una oficina, así que trabaja en su tienda local al aire libre. Ella guarda su cheque de pago y se pone a hablar de su hobby favorito todo el día: acampar.

Todos los sábados, Molly trabaja en el **segundo** piso, con todas las tiendas de campaña, mochilas y suministros para acampar. Este sábado, entra su **primo**.

"¡Hola, Jim!", dice Molly, una sonrisa feliz en su rostro.

"¡Molly! Olvidé que trabajas aquí", dice Jim, el **hijo** de **treinta** años de la **tía** de Molly, Jane.

"¿Cómo están la tía Jane y el **tío** Joe?", pregunta Molly.

"Están bien. Este fin de semana están visitando a la **abuela** Gloria en su casa", dice Jim. "Estoy aquí para comprar algunos productos al aire libre para un viaje."

"¡Oh, claro! Puedo ayudarte. ¿Qué hay en tu lista?" pregunta Molly.

Jim le muestra a Molly un pedazo de papel con una lista de **quince** artículos. Una mochila ligera, una estufa portátil, cuatro pares de calcetines calientes, bastones de senderismo, el jabón mágico del Dr. Bronner, un cuchillo de bolsillo y **dieciocho** comidas deshidratadas.

Vaya, esto suena como un viaje, piensa Molly.

"Dame la mochila más ligera que tengas", dice Jim. "La más ligera de todo, en realidad. Tengo que mantener mi mochila por debajo de **veintiocho** libras."

"¿Para qué estás comprando todo esto?", pregunta Molly, caminando con Jim hacia una pared llena de mochilas de todos los colores, grandes y pequeñas.

"Voy a caminar", dice Jim. "Por toda España."

Jim prueba las diferentes mochilas. Elige la favorita de Molly, una mochila roja con **siete** bolsillos, cuatro en la espalda y tres en el interior. El paquete es tan ligero, que apenas pesa **dos libras y media**. Lo lleva sobre sus hombros mientras sigue a Molly a la sección de ropa.

"Se llama el Camino de Santiago", le dice Jim a Molly. Su primo le habla de la caminata. Es una peregrinación a la Catedral de Santiago de Compostela en Galicia. Se dice que Santiago está enterrado en la iglesia.

www.LearnLikeNatives.com

El tío Jim caminará la caminata desde el punto de partida común de la Vía Francesa, Saint-Jean-Pied-de-Port. A partir de ahí, son unas **quinientas** millas hasta Santiago. La peregrinación ha sido popular desde la Edad Media. Los criminales y otras personas caminaban por el camino a cambio de bendiciones. Hoy en día, la mayoría viaja a pie. Algunas personas viajan en bicicleta. Algunos peregrinos incluso viajan a caballo o en burro. La peregrinación era religiosa, pero ahora muchos la hacen para viajar o para hacer deporte.

"Necesito viajar", dice Jim. "Necesito tiempo para pensar y reflexionar. Caminar 500 millas puede ser muy espiritual."

Molly ayuda a Jim a encontrar una chaqueta impermeable y un par de pantalones que pueden descomprimirse para ser pantalones cortos. Parece muy feliz con su gran bolsa de cosas. Él tiene mucho más en sus manos que los otros compradores. Él va en un viaje real.

"Serán **trescientos cuarenta y siete** dólares y **sesenta y seis** centavos", dice Molly.

"Gracias, Molly", dice Jim.

Molly empieza a pensar. Vive en casa con sus **padres**. Su madre trabaja como juez en el juzgado local y su padre es abogado. Ambos raramente están en casa para cenar. Permanecen ocupados en la oficina hasta tarde. Sus **hermanos** viven con sus familias en Seattle, a tres horas de distancia. Está sola, sin trabajo de verdad. No tiene a nadie que la detenga.

Serán unas vacaciones perfectas. Y quizás ella decida qué hacer con el resto de su vida.

¿Por qué no?

Ese día, Mollly decide que hará el Camino de Santiago. A partir de septiembre, dentro de tres meses. Sola.

RESUMEN

Una joven llamada Molly ama el aire libre. Ella y su familia acampan juntos a menudo. Trabaja en una tienda al aire libre mientras busca trabajo después de la universidad. Su tío Jim la visita para prepararse para un viaje. Va a caminar por el Camino de Santiago y necesita suministros. Molly le ayuda a comprar una mochila, zapatos y todo lo que necesita. Ella misma decide tomar el camino.

www.LearnLikeNatives.com

Lista de Vocabulario

family	familia
two	dos
brother	hermano
sister	hermana
one	una
three	tres
mom	mamá
dad	papá
eight	ocho
nineteen	diecinueve
twenty	veinte
mother	madre
father	padre
twenty-two	veintidós
second	segundo

cousin	primo
thirty	treinta
son	hijo
aunt	tía
uncle	tío
grandma	abuela
fifteen	quince
four	cuatro
eighteen	dieciocho
twenty-eight	veintiocho
seven	siete
two-and-a-half	dos y medio
five hundred	quinientos
three hundred	trescientos
forty-seven	cuarenta y siete
sixty-six	sesenta y seis

parents	padres
siblings	hermanos

PREGUNTAS

1) ¿Qué estudió Molly en la universidad?

    a) cosmetología

    b) literatura

    c) ingeniería

    d) comercialización

2) ¿Cuántos hermanos tiene Molly?

    a) uno

    b) dos

    c) tres

    d) cuatro

3) ¿Qué relación tiene Jim con Molly?

    a) hermano

    b) tío

    c) abuelo

    d) papá

4) ¿Qué es el Camino de Santiago?

    a) una peregrinación

    b) una ciudad

    c) una iglesia

    d) un día de fiesta

5) ¿De dónde es Molly?

    a) Estados Unidos

    b) Inglaterra

c) Australia

d) Francia

RESPUESTAS

1) ¿Qué estudió Molly en la universidad?

   c) ingeniería

2) ¿Cuántos hermanos tiene Molly?

   c) tres

3) ¿Qué relación tiene Jim con Molly?

   b) tío

4) ¿Qué es el Camino de Santiago?

a) una peregrinación

5) ¿De dónde es Molly?

a) Estados Unidos

Translation of the Story

The Camino Inspiration

Molly loves adventures.

She is the bravest member of her **family**, even braver than her **two brothers**. She often goes camping with her family in the woods. This weekend, they go to the mountain together. The moon shines and the birds and animals are quiet. Molly sits with her brothers and her **sister** by the fire, talking and playing. They see a bat fly over their heads.

"Ewww!" shouts Molly's sister.

"A bat!" yells **one** of Molly's brothers.

Then, **three** more bats fly over their heads.

"Ahhh! Let's get **mom** and **dad**!" shouts the other brother, John.

"It's only a bat," says Molly.

More bats arrive, until there are **eight** flying overhead. Molly's sister and brothers disappear into their tents, scared out of their wits. Molly does not move. She watches as the bats circled, now **nineteen**, no, **twenty**!

"Hi, Molly," says her **mother**, walking up behind her **father** to the campfire.

"Wow, there sure are a lot of bats around these woods," says her dad. "Aren't you scared?"

Molly shook her head no, and watched the bats fly off into the starry night sky.

"Let's eat dinner!" she said. Her brothers and sister come out of their tents. The family eats by the fire. They love to camp together.

Molly is **twenty-two**. She just graduated from college, where she studied engineering. She has not found a job in an office, so she works at her local outdoor store. She saves her paycheck and gets to talk about her favorite hobby all day: camping.

Every Saturday, Molly works on the **second** floor, with all of the tents, backpacks, and camping supplies. This Saturday, in walks her **cousin**.

"Hi, Jim!" says Molly, a happy smile on her face.

"Molly! I forgot you work here," says Jim, the **thirty**-year-old **son** of Molly's **aunt** Jane.

"How are Aunt Jane and **Uncle** Joe?" asks Molly.

"They're good. This weekend they are visiting **Grandma** Gloria at her house," says Jim. "I'm here to buy some outdoor goods for a trip."

"Oh, sure! I can help you. What is on your list?" Molly asks.

Jim shows Molly a piece of paper with a list of **fifteen** items. A light backpack, a portable stove, **four** pairs of warm socks, hiking poles, Dr. Bronner's magic soap, a pocket knife, and **eighteen** dehydrated trail meals.

Wow, this sounds like quite a trip, thinks Molly.

"Gimme the lightest backpack you have," says Jim. "The lightest everything, actually. I have to keep my pack under **twenty-eight** pounds."

"What are you buying all of this for?" asks Molly, walking with Jim over to a wall filled with backpacks of all colors, large and small.

"I'm going to hike," says Jim. "Across Spain."

Jim tries on the different backpacks. He chooses Molly's favorite, a red backpack with **seven** pockets, four on the back and three inside. The pack is so light, it hardly weighs **two-and-a-half** pounds. He wears it on his shoulders as he follows Molly to the clothing section.

"It's called the Camino de Santiago," Jim tells Molly. Her cousin tells her about the hike. It is a pilgrimage to the Cathedral of Santiago de Compostela in Galicia. People say that Saint James is buried in the church.

Uncle Jim will be walking the hike from the common starting point of the French Way, Saint-Jean-Pied-de-Port. From there, it is about **five hundred** miles to Santiago. The pilgrimage has been popular since the Middle Ages. Criminals and other people walked the way in exchange for blessings. Nowadays, most travel by foot. Some people travel by bicycle. A few pilgrims even travel on a horse or donkey. The pilgrimage was religious, but now many do it for travel or sport.

"I need to travel," says Jim. "I need time to think and reflect. Walking 500 miles can be very spiritual."

Molly helps Jim find a waterproof jacket and a pair of pants that can unzip to be shorts. He seems very happy with his large bag of things. He has much more in his hands than the other shoppers. He is going on a real trip.

"That will be **three hundred forty-seven** dollars and **sixty-six** cents," says Molly.

"Thanks, Molly," says Jim.

Molly begins to think. She lives at home with her **parents**. Her mother works as a judge in the local courthouse and her father is a lawyer. They are both rarely home for dinner. They stay busy at the office until late. Her **siblings** live with their families in Seattle, three hours away. She is alone, with no real job. She has no one to stop her.

It will be the perfect vacation. And maybe she will decide what to do with the rest of her life.

Why not?

That day, Mollly decides that she will do the Camino de Santiago. Starting in September, three months from now. Alone.

www.LearnLikeNatives.com

www.LearnLikeNatives.com

CONCLUSION

You did it!

You finished a whole book in a brand new language. That in and of itself is quite the accomplishment, isn't it?

Congratulate yourself on time well spent and a job well done. Now that you've finished the book, you have familiarized yourself with over 500 new vocabulary words, comprehended the heart of 3 short stories, and listened to loads of dialogue unfold, all without going anywhere!

Charlemagne said "To have another language is to possess a second soul." After immersing yourself in this book, you are broadening your horizons and opening a whole new path for yourself.

Have you thought about how much you know now that you did not know before? You've learned everything from how to greet and how to express your emotions to basics like colors and place words. You can tell time and ask question. All without opening a schoolbook. Instead, you've cruised through fun, interesting stories and possibly listened to them as well.

Perhaps before you weren't able to distinguish meaning when you listened to Spanish. If you used the audiobook, we bet you can now pick out meanings and words when you hear someone speaking. Regardless, we are sure you have taken an important step to being more fluent. You are well on your way!

Best of all, you have made the essential step of distinguishing in your mind the idea that most often hinders people studying a new language. By approaching Spanish through our short stories and dialogs, instead of formal lessons with just grammar and vocabulary, you are no longer in the 'learning' mindset. Your approach is much more similar to an osmosis, focused on speaking and using the language, which is the end goal, after all!

So, what's next?

This is just the first of five books, all packed full of short stories and dialogs, covering essential, everyday Spanish that will ensure you master the basics. You can find the rest of the books in the series, as well as a whole host of other resources, at LearnLikeNatives.com. Simply add the book to your library to take the next step in your language learning journey. If you are ever in need of new ideas or direction, refer to our 'Speak Like a Native' eBook, available to you for free at LearnLikeNatives.com, which clearly outlines practical steps you can take to continue learning any language you choose.

www.LearnLikeNatives.com

We also encourage you to get out into the real world and practice your Spanish. You have a leg up on most beginners, after all—instead of pure textbook learning, you have been absorbing the sound and soul of the language. Do not underestimate the foundation you have built reviewing the chapters of this book. Remember, no one feels 100% confident when they speak with a native speaker in another language.

One of the coolest things about being human is connecting with others. Communicating with someone in their own language is a wonderful gift. Knowing the language turns you into a local and opens up your world. You will see the reward of learning languages for many years to come, so keep that practice up!. Don't let your fears stop you from taking the chance to use your Spanish. Just give it a try, and remember that you will make mistakes. However, these mistakes will teach you so much, so view every single one as a small victory! Learning is growth.

www.LearnLikeNatives.com

Don't let the quest for learning end here! There is so much you can do to continue the learning process in an organic way, like you did with this book. Add another book from Learn Like a Native to your library. Listen to Spanish talk radio. Watch some of the great Spanish films. Put on the latest

CD from Rosalia. Take salsa lessons in Spanish. Whatever you do, don't stop because every little

step you take counts towards learning a new language, culture, and way of communicating.

www.LearnLikeNatives.com

www.LearnLikeNatives.com

www.LearnLikeNatives.com

Learn Like a Native is a revolutionary **language education brand** that is taking the linguistic world by storm. Forget boring grammar books that never get you anywhere, Learn Like a Native teaches you languages in a fast and fun way that actually works!

As an international, multichannel, language learning platform, we provide **books, audio guides and eBooks** so that you can acquire the knowledge you need, swiftly and easily.

Our **subject-based learning**, structured around real-world scenarios, builds your conversational muscle and ensures you learn the content most relevant to your requirements.
Discover our tools at ***LearnLikeNatives.com***.

When it comes to learning languages, we've got you covered!

www.ingramcontent.com/pod-product-compliance
Lightning Source LLC
Chambersburg PA
CBHW071747080526
44588CB00013B/2176